Teddy Needs a Bath

Teddy Needs a Bath

Danielle Bernard

Teddy the cat, was fluffy and soft.

He was black and white, with a sprinkle of brown.

His tail was so fluffy, like a fox in the snow.

He swirled and swished it wherever he would go.

He sniffed in the garden and rolled in the mud,

He chased a bug, then tumbled into a puddle, and a muddy wet slug!

"Oh, Teddy!" gasped Elle. "You are smelly and wet!"

Teddy looked puzzled, and gave a small "Meow".

Splish and splash went the water, and the bubbles went pop!

Teddy tried to wriggle, but Elle said "Stop!"

Teddy now wrapped in a towel, he licked his wet fur.

He licked his tail until it was fluffy, which made him purr!

At last he was shiny, clean, soft and bright.

He curled by the fire, all fluffy and warm.

He looked out the window and thought,

I'll stay clear of that storm!

The very next morning, can you guess what he did?

He rolled in the mud, he fell into another puddle....

Then he quickly hid!

About a clumsy cat named Teddy, who lives in Australia.

| 14 | -

www.ingramcontent.com/pod-product-compliance
Lightning Source LLC
Chambersburg PA
CBHW051216290426
44109CB00021B/2474